BrAiN BENDERS

NOT SO ORDINARY

Thanks to the creative team:

Senior Editor: Alice Peebles

Designer: Bryony Anne Warren and Collaborate Agency

First American edition published in 2015 by Lerner Publishing Group, Inc.

Hungry Tomato™
A division of Lerner Publishing Group, Inc.
241 First Avenue North
Minneapolis, MN 55401 USA

For reading levels and more information, look up this title at www.lernerbooks.com.

The Cataloging-in-Publication Data for *Not So Ordinary* is on file at the Library of Congress.
ISBN 978-1-4677-6347-9 (lib. bdg.)
ISBN 978-1-4677-7199-3 (pbk.)
ISBN 978-1-4677-7200-6 (EB pdf)

Manufactured in the United States of America
1 – VP – 7/15/15

NOT SO ORDINARY

by Dr. Gareth Moore

HUNGRY TOMATO™

MINNEAPOLIS

Contents

Not So Ordinary

Who says you need a phone or a computer to banish boredom? For this collection of household challenges, you can use everyday objects to take on perplexing puzzles and tricky tasks. At the back of the book, you'll find tips to help you with each challenge, plus an answers section that explains how everything works. And once you've solved these challenges, you can come up with some of your own activities using the same objects. So take a seat, get comfortable, and have fun using ordinary items to create extraordinary fun.

Dice decision

For this trick you'll need three dice, which you could borrow from a couple of board games if you don't have any handy. You'll also need a drinking glass or some other object that you can see through from underneath.

Ask a friend to drop the three dice into a glass, then hold it up, look through the bottom, and add up the numbers he or she can see on the dice. Your friend shouldn't let you see the numbers or tell you the total.

Now have your friend pass you the glass. Without looking underneath, you can instantly guess your friend's total. Magic!

To do this trick, just add up the numbers on top of the three dice and subtract this sum from 21. That's the total your friend counted on the underside of the dice. So if the total on top of the dice was 15, you would calculate 21 - 15 to make 6, which was your friend's answer!

Why does this trick always work?

Need help with solving these puzzles? Turn to pages 26 – 28 for helpful tips.

5

Easy Jaw-Droppers

These amazing tricks don't call for any special equipment, just common items that you or a friend will probably have. On these pages, for example, you need just your hands, your eyes, and a piece of paper!

1 The vanishing color

Close your right eye, and hold this book as far out in front of you as you can.

You can see all three of these colored discs below, as you would expect.

Now look at the blue disc on the right-hand side and slowly move the book toward you, keeping your right eye closed the whole time.

As the book gets closer, a funny thing happens. First, the red disc disappears!

If you look at the red disc directly, it will appear again, so keep looking at the blue disc. You will see it disappear out of the corner of your eye.

Now keep moving the book closer. All of a sudden the red disc reappears, and the green disc disappears instead!

Can you explain why this happens?

2 Square dance

Can you explain it ?

Find a square-shaped piece of paper and cut it into the four shapes shown here.

Start by making the diagonal cut along the edge of the yellow shape. Then cut the top piece in two along the vertical line. Finally, cut the top left piece in two.

Now rearrange the four shapes like this...

Why does rearranging the shapes mean that one of them doesn't fit into the square anymore?

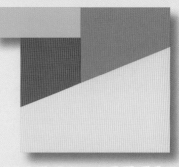

3 An extra finger

Can you make a ghostly third finger appear to float in front of your face, as shown here? The secret is to hold your hands in a particular position relative to your eyes. Can you figure out where?

Need help with solving these puzzles? Turn to pages 26 – 28 for helpful tips.

Matchstick Challenges

You might have come across "matchstick" puzzles before. The goal is to rearrange a set of matches in a particular way. You don't need to have any actual matches for these games, though. You can use pens or pencils, straws, or even blades of grass to try it yourself!

1 Matching squares

Start by laying out your "matchsticks" as shown here.

This is the challenge: can you remove just **two** matches to leave only two squares and no matches that aren't part of a square? You aren't allowed to touch any of the other matches!

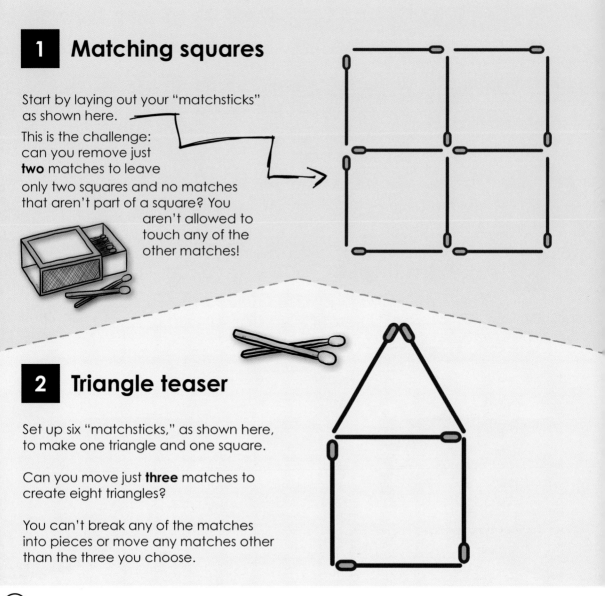

2 Triangle teaser

Set up six "matchsticks," as shown here, to make one triangle and one square.

Can you move just **three** matches to create eight triangles?

You can't break any of the matches into pieces or move any matches other than the three you choose.

3   Something fishy

Arrange your "matchsticks" as shown here, so that they look like a fish swimming to the left.

By moving just **three** matchsticks, can you make the fish swim to the right?

The new fish should look like the mirror image of the first fish.

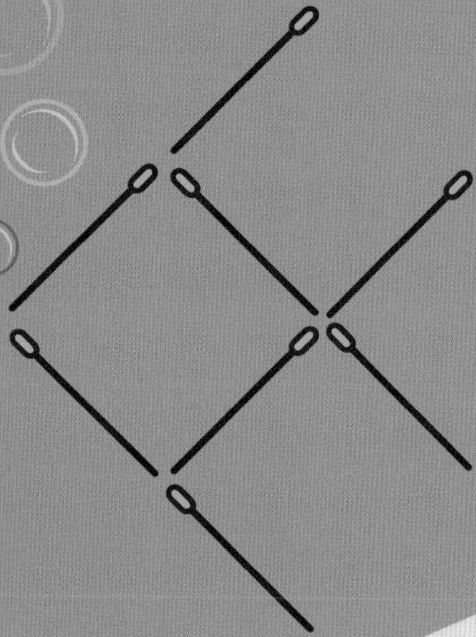

4   Stick numbers

Lay out your "matchsticks" so that they look like the problem "4 – 3 = " as shown here. Can you move **three** matches to make a valid equation, so that what's on the left of the equals sign is equal to the value on the right?

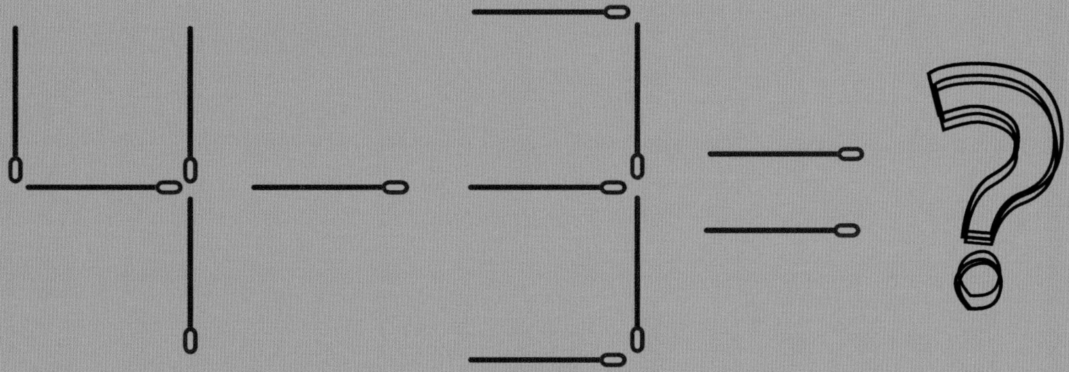

Need help with solving these puzzles? Turn to pages 26 – 28 for helpful tips.

Puzzles with Coins

To solve the puzzles on these two pages, you'll need some pennies or counters—or even scraps of paper: anything about the size of a penny that will cover one of the puzzle squares. You may find it easier to re-draw these puzzles on a sheet of paper, so that coins can comfortably fit over the squares in each puzzle.

1 Maze of no repeats

For each of these puzzles, place pennies (or similar items that fit) over some of the numbers so that no number can be seen more than once in any row or column. You must place them so that the squares without pennies remain connected, like the paths in a maze. That way you can travel from one empty square to another empty square just by sliding an extra coin around the finished puzzle. (Squares that only touch diagonally don't count as connected.)

Here's an example of a solved puzzle. The "coins" are slightly transparent so that you can see the numbers underneath. Notice how all the squares without coins are connected in one area.

1	3	1
1	2	3
3	3	1

3	3	2
2	1	3
3	1	2

3	3	1
1	2	1
3	1	3

4	2	3	4
1	3	4	2
1	2	1	4
2	4	1	4

2 Submarine search

The aim of this game is to find the hidden fleet of submarines and place a coin on each square that hides a submarine. The shaded squares with numbers on them are islands. Each island's number gives the total count of all the submarines in the row and column where the island is. Submarines can't touch either each other or an island, not even diagonally.

Take a look at this example below. Notice how the 2 at the bottom left is correct because you'll get a total of two ships when you count up the column and along the row where the island is located. Also notice how none of the ships touch either each other or an island. Now try it for yourself!

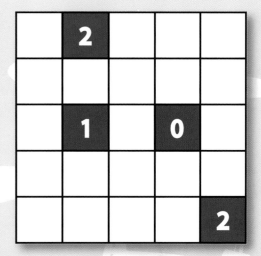

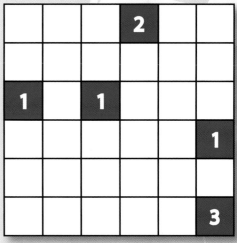

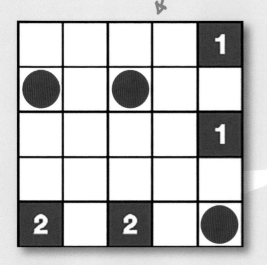

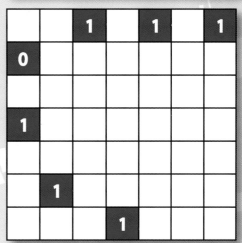

Need help with solving these puzzles? Turn to pages 26 – 28 for helpful tips.

Coin Games

You can do a lot of things with coins besides spend them! Magicians sometimes use them for tricks, but on these pages you'll look at other creative ways you can use them – without leaving your chair.

1 Moving coins

You'll need six coins for this puzzle. Start by arranging them on the table so that they look like the coins on the left:

Can you rearrange them in just three moves to make a hexagon, so that they look like the picture on the right?

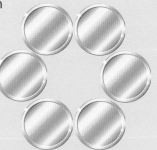

It sounds easy, but you can only slide coins along the table instead of picking them up, which means that if a coin is blocked by another one, you can't move it.

There's one other rule: whenever you finish sliding a coin, you always have to leave it so that it is touching exactly two other coins. Good luck!

2 Touching coins

Here's another coin game that depends on how many times coins touch each other. Set out four coins like this:

Can you figure out how to rearrange those coins so that every coin is touching all three other coins?

3 Tossing a coin

Have you ever tossed a coin to choose heads or tails? Professional sports players sometimes do this before a game to decide who begins play – in a tennis match, for example.

The sides of a coin are large in comparison to its edge, so when you throw it up in the air, you can be pretty certain it will land on one of its sides, not its narrow edge. You probably can't even balance a coin on its edge, unless it's really thick.

Since it's so extremely unlikely that a coin will ever land on its edge, the "probability" of this is 0%. Probability is how likely something is to happen. A probability of 100% means something will definitely happen no matter what. A probability of 0% means something will never happen no matter what. For most events, probability is a percentage between 0 and 100. So a 50% probability means an event is one of two possible outcomes, both equally likely.

When you toss a coin, there are two possible outcomes: it lands on heads or it lands on tails. These two outcomes are equally likely, so the probability of each is 50%. But that doesn't mean that if you toss a coin 30 times, it will land on heads 15 times and tails 15 times. Each time you toss the coin, you have a 50% chance of either outcome. In other words, it doesn't matter what the previous result was – on each throw the probability of heads or of tails is always 50%. If you're not convinced of this, try it and write down the result after each toss.

Next, try this challenge. If you toss two coins at the same time, what is the probability that both will land on heads or both on tails? First, think about the various possibilities and figure out what you expect the result to be. Then try it out 40 times with the coins, keeping a count of how many times you get both heads or both tails. How often does this happen? Is it about a quarter (25%), a third (33%), or half (50%) of the time? Does this match what you expected?

Need help with solving these puzzles? Turn to pages 26 – 28 for helpful tips.

Card Conundrums

You'll need a pack of playing cards to try the games on these pages. If you can't find a pack of normal playing cards, special cards from any other game that uses cards will work.

1 The magic card

First, count out 27 cards and put the rest of the deck away. Make sure all the cards are different, or this trick won't work!

Deal a row of three cards, face up, from left to right. Keep dealing more rows of three cards until you have three columns of cards, each made up of nine rows. Each row of cards should overlap the previous row a little, so that you can pick up a column without changing the order of the cards.

Next, ask a friend to secretly choose a card and only tell you which column it is in. Slide each column into its own pile, and then reassemble the piles so that the pile with your friend's card goes in the middle. Once you have all the cards back in a single pile, turn the pile over so that the cards are face down in your hands.

Now repeat the whole process, dealing from the top of the deck and turning the cards over as you go so that they are face up again. Again ask your friend to pick a pile, and again pick up the three piles in such a way that your friend's pile goes in the middle. Try not to make it obvious that you are doing this!

Finally, repeat everything for a third time: deal all the cards, ask for the column, and reassemble the cards into a face-down pile with your friend's in the middle of the stack. Here's where the magic comes in. Your friend's card is guaranteed to be the 14th card in the pack, counting down from the top. Deal the cards out and keep a secret count in your head. Once you get to the 14th card, you can stop and ask if it's your friend's card. Amazingly, it will be!

2   Card placement

Here's a card puzzle you can try with a pencil and paper – you don't need actual playing cards.

Try to figure out how to place the four listed playing cards into this grid so that the following statements are all true:

- The red cards are both in the same row.
- In one of the columns, if you add up both card values, the result is equal to the value of a single card in the other column.
- In both columns, a lower value card is at the bottom.
- In the top row, the card on the left is lower in value than the card on the right.

Can you re-draw the box with the correct cards in it?

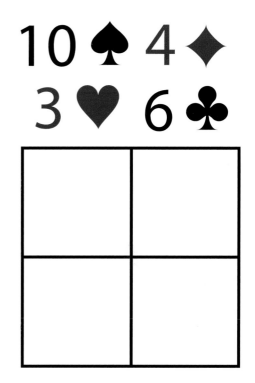

3   Card memory

For this game, a deck of regular playing cards works best. Remove all the black cards, so you only have the red ones left. You will now have two of each value: two aces, two 2s, and so on. (If you don't have regular playing cards, you'll need a deck with some pairs of cards that you consider equal in some way.) Shuffle the cards and deal them face down in two rows of 13 cards each.

Turn over any two cards. If they have the same value, remove them and put them to the side. If they don't match in value, turn them back over so that you can't see their values. Keep doing this – turning over two cards and removing them if they match, and turning them back over if they don't. How many attempts does it take to remove them all?

This game is a great memory test, so it's well worth practicing and playing more than once. You can also play with a friend and take turns turning over cards to see who can remove the most pairs!

Need help with solving these puzzles? Turn to pages 26 – 28 for helpful tips.

Sliding Block Puzzles

You might have played with sliding block puzzles before, but have you ever made your own? All you need is a piece of cardboard and this book!

Take a piece of cardboard and copy these colored shapes as accurately as you can. Try to make them the exact same size as they are on this page. You might find this easier if you use a ruler. There's no need to color the shapes if you don't want to, but you might find it helpful.

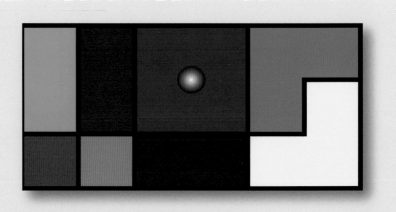

Cut out your eight shapes along the thick black lines. Now you're ready for these next challenges! There are three in order of increasing difficulty, and you won't need all the pieces until the last challenge.

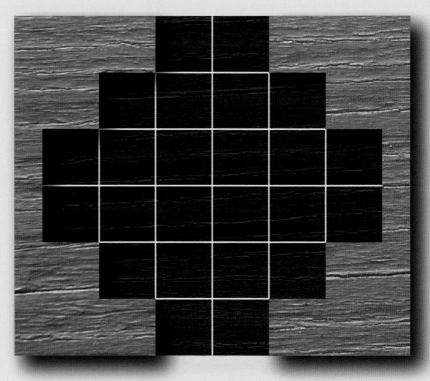

1 Sliding around

Start by arranging your pieces exactly like this on the empty wooden board. The large red square, marked with the brown dot, is at the top of the puzzle. By sliding the pieces around, can you move the red square to the bottom of the puzzle so that it will escape through the gap? Pieces can only be moved into areas on the dark part of the puzzle – they can't move onto the light outer wood. You can move a piece by sliding it horizontally or vertically, but never diagonally. Pieces must stay in the white lines, so each one always ends up touching another piece, a white line, or the edge of the play area. And the pieces must not overlap in any way!

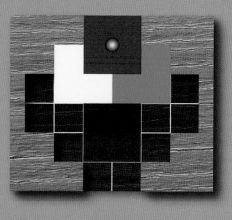

2 Sliding further

Now try this trickier challenge!

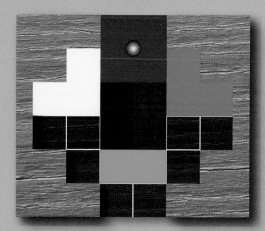

3 The ultimate challenge

If you managed to complete the first two puzzles, see if you can solve this monster puzzle. It will take a lot of moves to get the red square to the bottom!

You can also try making up your own puzzles. You could even design your own shapes for the pieces.

Need help with solving these puzzles? Turn to pages 26 – 28 for helpful tips.

Paper Challenges

You can invent all sorts of brain teasers with a few pieces of paper. For the activities on these pages you'll need plenty of paper to cut up, plus a pair of scissors.

1 Through the page

Can you walk through a hole in a piece of paper? Probably not, unless the piece of paper is incredibly large and you cut a really big hole! But there is a secret method that lets you walk through a normal-sized piece of paper, such as a page from a notebook.

Fold the piece of paper in half, as shown in the first diagram below. Then make alternating cuts in the paper as shown by the bold red lines in the second diagram. The more cuts you can fit in, the better, but make sure you don't cut all the way across to make two separate pieces of paper!

Finally, cut along the fold, being careful not to cut the very first or the very last strip of paper. Now unfold the paper – and step right through it!

1

2

3

2 A single cut

You'll need a square of paper for this activity. (If you need to, cut a rectangular piece to make it square.) Did you know you can cut interesting shapes in a piece of paper even with a **single** straight cut through it? The secret is in how you fold it first.

1

Try this out by folding a square of paper diagonally in half, then diagonally in half again, as shown in the first two pictures below. Finally, make one single cut across the point of the resulting triangle, like in the third picture.

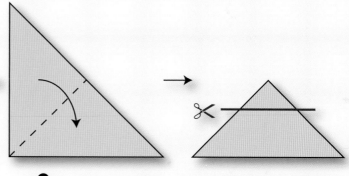

2

Now unfold the paper. You'll have a diamond in the middle, like this:

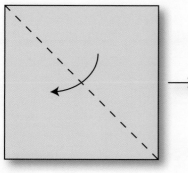

3

Using this simple trick, you can make all kinds of interesting shapes and patterns. Now here's the challenge: can you work out how to get the following results, just by folding a square of paper and again making **only one** cut?

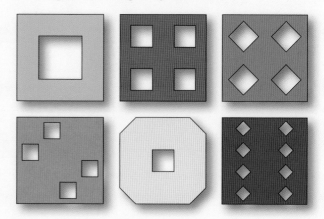

Need help with solving these puzzles? Turn to pages 26 – 28 for helpful tips.

More Paper Games

We're just beginning to explore the folding magic of paper. On these pages you'll use paper to tell the future and create a shape-making puzzle.

1 Future folding

Have you ever made a paper fortune-teller? It's easy to make and fun to play with!

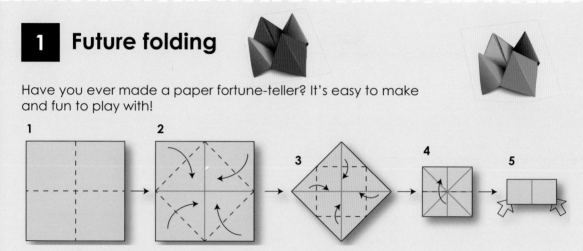

Fold a square of paper in half both ways, as shown. Fold the four corners into the center, and then fold the resulting set of corners into the center. Finally, fold the paper in half and insert your fingers and thumbs into the four pockets you've created underneath. Now spread your fingers apart to complete your fortune-teller.

There are four petals folded into the hole on the top of the fortune-teller. Unfold one petal and write "yes" on the underside. Fold the petal back in. Repeat with the other three petals, writing "no," "maybe," and "ask again."

Now you can answer any question! Get a friend to ask a question about the future and give you a number between 10 and 20. Insert your fingers into the four pockets underneath the fortune-teller, and open and close it in an alternating direction on each count. Then ask your friend to pick one of the two petals that are visible at the end of the count, and that's the answer to the question!

2   Pattern placement

Copy the following arrangement of shapes onto a piece of cardboard. You will find it easier to do this if you start by drawing the outside of the square. Then draw the internal dividing lines. After that, cut out the whole square, and finally cut out the eight individual pieces.

Now, simply by arranging the pieces, can you create each of the pictures shown in silhouette? The pieces shouldn't overlap at all. And don't turn over any pieces. (Keep them colored-side up if you color-coded them.)

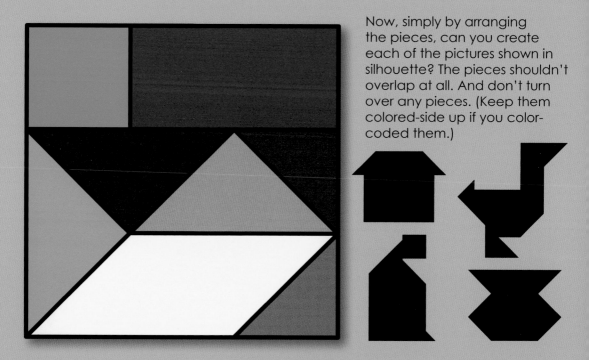

3   Folding issue

How many times can you fold a piece of paper in half without unfolding it in between? Make a guess before you try it out. Does it matter what size the paper is? If you have a piece of paper that's twice as large as a regular sheet of paper, can you make twice as many folds? Can some kinds of paper be folded more than others?

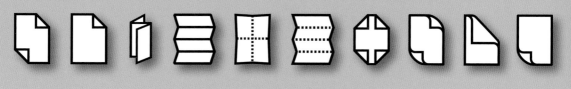

Need help with solving these puzzles? Turn to pages 26 – 28 for helpful tips.

Fun with Objects

To try out the activities on these pages you'll need a variety
of objects from around the house!

1 Pre-sliced banana

Have you ever peeled and sliced a banana or had someone slice a banana
for you? Wouldn't it be amazing if you could peel a banana and find that it was
already sliced? It would certainly be a neat trick to play on a friend.

Here's how to do it. You need a very clean needle, about 1 foot (30 cm) of
thread, a banana, and help or permission from an adult.

The needle should be at least as long as
the banana is thick. Once the needle is
threaded, use it to sew a square shape
around the inside of the banana, just
under the surface of the skin.

To do this, push the needle through one
side of the banana and out the other
side, as close to the outer edge of the banana as possible, making sure you leave
thread hanging out of the banana on both sides. Next, push the needle back
into the banana at the exact point where it just came out, and make the second
side of the square. Again, don't pull the end of the thread out of the banana yet.
Repeat on the third and fourth sides, until your needle comes back out of the hole
where you first started.

Now grab hold of both loose ends of the thread that are
sticking out of the banana, and pull them tight. This will
slice the banana inside its skin. You can then pull all the
thread out of the banana.

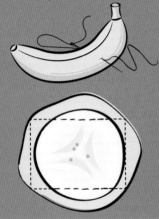

Repeat these steps until you've made as many slices
in the banana as you want. Then give the banana to
someone who doesn't know what you've done and
have that person peel it. *Voilà*, a pre-sliced banana!

2 Spaghetti bridge

It's easy to snap a piece of uncooked spaghetti in half, but is it always equally easy? In this activity you'll find out! You'll need a package of spaghetti and some tape, plus two boxes of similar height.

Set the boxes next to each other so that they are about 6 inches (15 cm) apart. Now place one strand of spaghetti across the gap between the boxes, and tape each end to the box it is resting on. You've now formed a single-strand bridge between the two boxes.

Press down gently with your finger on the middle of the spaghetti, in the gap halfway between the boxes. Keep pressing down until the spaghetti bends by about 2 inches (5 cm).

Amazingly, it doesn't snap! It just bends and then returns to its original shape when you remove your finger. (If you press too hard, you'll probably find that it comes untaped before it snaps!)

Now untape the spaghetti from one of the boxes, and move the boxes 3/4 in. (2 cm) closer together. Retape the spaghetti to the box and repeat the experiment. Can you still bend it just as far with one finger?

Keep moving the boxes closer together to shorten the spaghetti bridge until you find the point where the spaghetti finally breaks. This won't happen until the distance between the boxes is small enough.

First, find out what this distance is. Next, can you figure out why the spaghetti breaks only at shorter distances?

For a further investigation, tape ten pieces of spaghetti right next to each other across the gap.

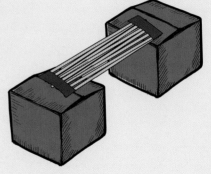

Can you still press your finger down on the spaghetti as easily as before?

Need help with solving these puzzles? Turn to pages 26 – 28 for helpful tips.

Games for Groups

You don't need to buy a fancy board game to play competitive games with friends! On these pages you'll make three of your own.

1 Target coins

You'll need a coin and a piece of paper for this game, which can be played with any number of people. Start by drawing a large target on the piece of paper, made up of circles of different sizes, as in the picture below. Write a number in each circle representing how many points it is worth, with the most points in the innermost circle. Place the paper target flat on a tabletop, about an arm's length from the edge of the table.

To play the game, roll a coin from the very edge of the table toward the target. If the coin stops on a line between any of the target rings, you score the number of points shown on the ring closer to the middle. Take turns rolling the coin. Decide in advance what the winning score will be, such as 25 points. The first person to reach that score is the winner. You can make the game more complex by drawing multiple targets on different pieces of paper, maybe even with different point amounts on them.

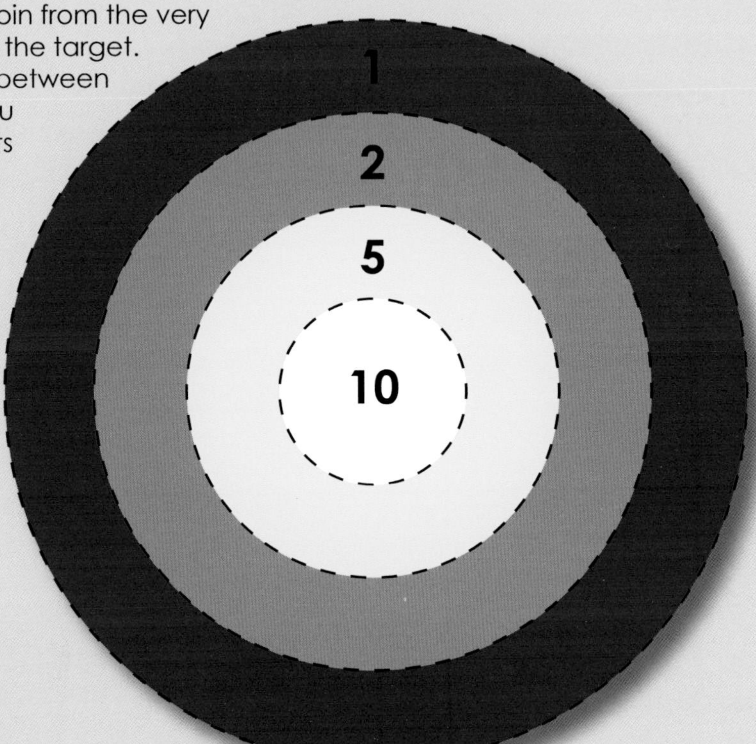

1

2

5

10

2 Pick up pencils

You'll need lots of pencils for this game, and they should be plain ones made of wood rather than mechanical pencils. The more pencils you have, the better! You can also play with as many people as you like. Start by dropping all the pencils on the floor in a random pile. If any land on their own, with no other pencils above or beneath them, move them onto the pile. You're now ready to start. Take turns removing a pencil from the pile. If a player removes a pencil from the pile without any other pencil moving, the player keeps that pencil. Otherwise the pencil goes into a discard pile. Keep going until there are no pencils left. The player with the most pencils at the end is the winner.

3 Last one loses

This game for two players is also played with pencils. (Or you can use pens, straws, or sticks if you wish.) Start by laying out the pencils in a row. Now, take turns removing one, two, or three pencils at a time. The winner is the player who has the last turn and picks up the last pencil. You can make the game more complicated by dividing the pencils into separate groups before you start. You then play in exactly the same way, except that you can only remove pencils from a single group each time you take a turn. The player to remove the last pencil from the last group is the winner.

Helpful Tips

Page 5

Not So Ordinary

Examine a die. What do you notice about the numbers on opposite sides?

Pages 6 – 7

Easy Jaw-Droppers

The vanishing color

Try repeating this trick with both eyes open. Do either of the objects still vanish? What does this tell you?

Square dance

Use a ruler to measure the dimensions of each square. Perhaps not all is as it seems!

An extra finger

If you move something really close to your face, does it start to look a little fuzzy? Does this give you a clue as to how you might create a ghostly floating finger?

Pages 8 – 9

Matchstick Challenges

Matching squares

In this setup, you have four squares that are all the same size. But the instructions don't say that both squares in the solution have to be the same size, do they?

Triangle teaser

Maybe you need to lay some of the matches on top of one another to make lots of small triangles.

Something fishy

When you change the direction of the fish, it will also shift up or down the page a bit.

Stick numbers

You know that the solution has to show the same value on either side of the equals sign, but you can't move many matches. Can you move the equals sign instead?

Pages 10 – 11

Puzzles with Coins

A maze of no repeats

The middle column has two 1's, which means that one of them must be covered. Try both options. You'll find that covering the middle square of the puzzle doesn't work, so you must have to cover the other one.

3	3	2
2	1	3
3	1	2

Submarine search

Every time you place a coin, you get rid of lots of other options, because coins can't touch one another. In the puzzle at the top of the page, there are only two squares where you can place coins that will be visible from the "2" island in the first row without breaking the rules, so you can place these two coins immediately.

Once you've done that, count how many coins are visible from the other islands. Are you finished already?

Pages 12 – 13

Coin Games

Moving coins

For the coins to end up in the right shape, one of the two coins in the center will have to move. You don't want it to get trapped, so move it as soon as you can.

Touching coins

Try picking up coins. This puzzle is much easier if you use actual coins or counters, instead of thinking about it with a piece of paper!

Tossing a coin

What results are possible when you toss two coins at the same time? You might get heads for the first coin and tails for the second, or tails for the first and heads for the second, for example. What other options are there? Are the options all equally likely?

Page 15

Card Conundrums

Card placement

You know that both red cards are in the same row, so the 3 and the 4 go on the same row. You also know that the lower value card is at the bottom, which means that the 3 and the 4 go on the bottom row and the 6 and the 10 go on the top row. Once you've figured out this much, the rest should be a little easier.

10♠ 4♦

3♥ 6♣

Pages 16 – 17

Sliding Block Puzzles

You need a little
patience to solve these.
If you get really confused,
move the pieces back to
the original arrangement
and try again. If you can
remember the positions
you've already tried, you
won't keep going in circles!

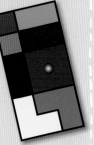

Page 19

Paper Challenges

A single cut

In the example you
folded the paper
diagonally in half and
then cut the point off. To
make all the other shapes,
you only need to fold
the paper horizontally,
vertically, or diagonally
in half – although you may
have to fold it two or more
times – and then make a cut.

Page 21

More Paper Games

Pattern placement

You only colored one side
of the card to remind you
that you can't turn over any
pieces, which means you only
have one option for the
yellow parallelogram.
If you get stuck, just
move on and try a
different picture.
You can also
make up your
own pictures
by arranging the
pieces in whatever ways you
want – or you can arrange them
randomly and then decide what
they look like!

Folding issue

You can vary the size of the
paper – and you can also vary
something else. What else varies
among different types of paper,
other than what's written or
printed on them?

Answers

Page 5 **Not So Ordinary**

The opposite sides of a die always add up to 7. This means that if you take the value on one side of a die and subtract it from 7, you find out the value on the other side. The trick hides this fact by using three dice, whose three sets of opposite sides must add up to 7 + 7 + 7 = 21. By subtracting the total of the top values from 21, we find out the total of the hidden values on the opposite sides.

An extra finger

Hold your two fingers apart and move them toward your eyes so they are only about 1 inch (3 cm) away. Between your eyes, just above your nose, you'll see a ghostly, floating "third finger." This is because your fingers are so close to your eyes that what you see with your left and right eyes is very different, and your brain finds it difficult to make sense of this.

Pages 6 – 7 **Easy Jaw-Droppers**

The vanishing color

The shapes vanish because each of your eyes has a blind spot where it can't see anything. Normally you aren't aware of this because everything in front of you can be seen by at least one of your eyes, so your brain can fill in the entire scene. That's why you need to close one eye for this to work. The blind spot is a region toward the center of each eye that has so many connections with your brain that there's no space for the part that looks out at the world. So, if the object you're looking at can only be seen by this part of your eye, it simply vanishes! Moving the book simply changes what is visible to your eye.

Square dance

The secret is that when the original square is reassembled into a square with a piece sticking out, the new square is not the same size as before. Measure the height of the original square and the height of the new square. You'll see that the new square is shorter! This reveals why one piece sticks out: because of the space missing from the top of the square. This area is highlighted here:

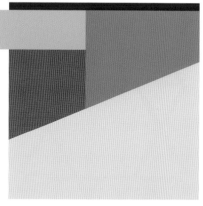

Matchstick Challenges

Matching squares

The two squares are different sizes, and they overlap each other:

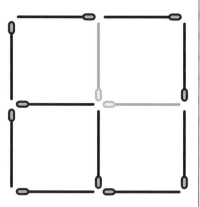

Triangle teaser

There are two sizes of triangle, and they again overlap each other:

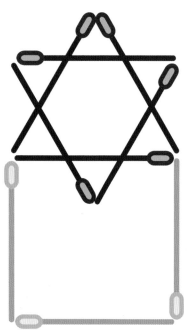

Puzzle with Coins

Maze of no repeats

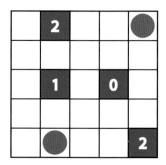

3	3	2
2	1	3
3	1	2

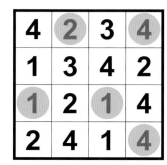

3	3	1
1	2	1
3	1	3

4	2	3	4
1	3	4	2
1	2	1	4
2	4	1	4

Submarine search

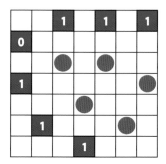

Something fishy

Stick numbers

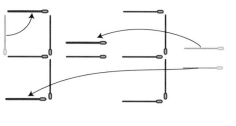

Coin Games

Moving coins

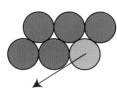

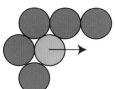

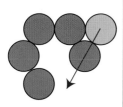

Folding issue

You probably figured out that you couldn't fold a piece of paper in half more than seven or eight times. It doesn't matter how big the original piece of paper is, because the problem isn't the size of the piece of paper. It's how thick the paper is. The more you fold it, the thicker it gets, and the harder it is to fold again.

Touching coins

The secret to this trick is to think in three dimensions! Arrange the coins as shown in this picture:

Page 15

Card Conundrum
Card placement

6 ♣	10 ♠
4 ♦	3 ♥

Page 21

More Paper Games
Pattern placement

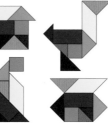

Tossing a coin

When you toss two coins together, the chance of them both being the same is 50%. You can work this out without testing it by thinking of the options, writing H for heads and T for tails:

H + H or H + T or T + T or T + H

There are four options, each equally likely (since there's a 50% chance any individual coin will land on heads and a 50% chance it will land on tails). Two of the four options have matching heads or tails. That's half of the total possible outcomes, or 50%.

Page 23

Fun with Objects
Spaghetti bridge

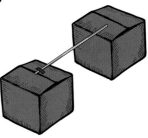

The longer the span of the bridge, the more you can bend the spaghetti before it snaps. The force you apply to a longer length of spaghetti gets spread out, so the pressure on any given point – where it might snap – is less. As you shorten the available length of spaghetti, the pressure on any given point increases and it becomes more likely to snap. Using ten pieces of spaghetti spreads the force from your finger over those ten strands, meaning that the pressure on each piece of spaghetti is roughly a tenth as strong. So you'll need to apply a lot more force to bend all the spaghetti as much as the single piece.

Index

About the Author

Dr Gareth Moore is the author of a wide range of puzzle and brain-training books for both children and adults, including *The Kids' Book of Puzzles*, *The Mammoth Book of Brain Games*, and *The Rough Guide Book of Brain Training*. He is also the founder of daily brain training site **www.BrainedUp.com**. He earned his Ph.D from Cambridge University (UK) in the field of computer speech recognition, teaching machines to understand spoken words.